The Art of Writing

Books of related interest by Sam Hamill

The Lotus Lovers (translations from Tzu Yeh and Li Ch'ing-chao)
Banished Immortal: Visions of Li T'ai-po
Facing the Snow: Visions of Tu Fu
A Dragon in the Clouds (poems and translations in the zen tradition)
Only Companion (poems from the Japanese)
Basho's Ghost (essays)
Basho's Oku no hosomichi (Narrow Road to the Interior)
A Poet's Work: The Other Side of Poetry (essays)

Lu Chi's *Wen Fu*

The Art of Writing

Translated by Sam Hamill

Revised Edition

MILKWEED EDITIONS

The Art of Writing
© 1991, Revised Translation and Introduction by Sam Hamill

Printed in the United States of America
Published in 1991 by *Milkweed Editions*
Post Office Box 3226
Minneapolis, Minnesota 55403
Books may be ordered at the above address

ISBN 0-915943-62-X

Publication of this book is made possible by grant support from the Literature Program of the National Endowment for the Arts, the Cowles Media / Star Tribune Foundation, the Dayton Hudson Foundation for Dayton's and Target Stores, the First Bank System Foundation, the General Mills Foundation, the I.A. O'Shaughnessy Foundation, the Jerome Foundation, the Minnesota State Arts Board through an appropriation by the Minnesota Legislature, the Northwest Area Foundation, and by the support of generous individuals.

Library of Congress Cataloging-in-Publication Data

Lu Chi, 261–303.
   [Wen fu. English]
   The art of writing : Lu Chi's Wen Fu / translated by Sam Hamill.
     p.   cm.
   Translation of: Wen fu.
   ISBN 0–915943–62–X : $6.95
   1. Chinese literature – History and criticism – Theory, etc.
  I. Hamill, Sam.
  PL2261.L8413 1991
  808'.04951 – dc20   90–25970
                                                                                CIP

An early version of this translation was first published by *The American Poetry Review*. First book publication (an edition limited to 200 copies) was that of Barbarian Press, Mission, in 1987, followed by a trade edition published by Breitenbush Books, also 1987.

For Ken Gerner and Mara Stahl

The Art of Writing

Introduction

In the history of Chinese letters, Lu Chi holds a position similar to that of Aristotle in the West, but with one paramount distinction: virtually every Chinese poet since the beginning of the fourth century has gone to school on the *Wen Fu*, and most memorized it. He is revered by traditionalist and experimentalist alike.

Lu Chi's *Wen Fu* is the first *ars poetica* of China and is composed in what might best be described as "prose poetry," except that it bears little or no resemblance to what passes as prose poetry in our own language. It is written in irregular poetic lines arranged as verse paragraphs rather like those used by Allen Ginsberg in *Howl*, but rhymed. While Lu Chi was not the inventor of the *fu* form, he put it to a striking new use, since before his time the *fu* was a popular form used for discursive poems on historical events or for singing the praises of one's military or political rulers.

Prior to the composition of the *Wen Fu*, the only truly great work to discuss the use of language is the *Ta Hsueh* (or *Great Learning*) of Kung-fu Tzu (Confucius). Master Kung believed all wisdom lay in learning to call things by the right name, and that only through the "rectification of names" might one proceed toward enlightened living. This insight is doubly remarkable when we remember that Kung-fu Tzu lived in a nation that was far more sophisticated than any other on earth at that time, its language rich in emblematic phrases, euphemisms, double-entendres, and layered ambiguities loaded with plurisignation. The *Ta Hsueh* is one of the "Stone Classics" carved around 175 A.D., late in the Han dynasty, in the capital city of Lo-yang. Initially, it was part of the *Li Chi* (*Book of Rites and Rituals*), but became a "book" in its own right nearly seven hundred years after Lu Chi would have studied it as part of his Confucian training during the late third century.

Lu Chi was born on the Yangtze Delta in 261 A.D., shortly after the end of Hellenistic Greece. It is impossible to learn whether Lu Chi knew or had heard about classical Greece, but he must have heard reports from the frontiers about the Roman Empire. And as an educated man, he was probably aware of the growth of Judeo-Christian civilization throughout his westernmost neighboring communities of "barbarians." He was a scholar of the *Analects* (*Lun Yu*) or dialogues of Master Kung, and of its precepts, many of which are echoed in the *Wen Fu*, −i.e. "How to play music may be known. At the commencement of the piece, all the parts should sound together. As it proceeds, they should be in harmony, while severally distinct and flowing without break, and thus on to conclusion." Or, "There are some who know all the notes, and there are some who know the music." Lu Chi owes a great deal, not only to the content of the *Lun Yu*, but to its very style, and to several of its more famous metaphors and similes.

Lu Chi was the grandson of Lu Sun, himself instrumental in attaining the southern throne for the first Wu emperor and who had been rewarded with the title of

Duke. Lu Chi's father was Lu K'ang, a military leader charged with responsibilities of protecting the empire from invaders from the north. The Lu family was itself from the north country, a family which had distinguished itself by producing military genius, men notable for their intense patriotism and reliability. Even so, Lu Sun's first passion was "to be a servant to the gods of the soil." Like his grandfather, Lu Chi held a deep abiding respect for the culture and landscape of the Yangtze Delta.

Lu K'ang had become a military leader at nineteen and had died when Lu Chi was twelve or thirteen, leaving six sons, at least three of whom, including Lu Chi, followed his example and entered the military. The Lu family estate was large and prosperous. They owned rice fields and mulberry groves along the delta, and bamboo groves in rolling hills near Hangchow Lake.

A strikingly large boy, Lu Chi grew to well over six feet. He was bright, and obsessed with learning. After his father died, he was named captain of the family troops and studied military strategy intensely for the ensuing five years. Despite Lu K'ang's many warnings about the threat of a major invasion from the north, the weak-willed Emperor Hao had neglected to reinforce the dwindling army, and when the invasion finally came, the Wu empire was decimated.

Two of Lu Chi's brothers were killed in battle, but both he and his beloved younger brother escaped and fled to Hua T'ing, where they "barred the door and devoted themselves to study." It is typical of Lu, and of Chinese genius in general, that in the face of utter defeat, he searches forsolutions within himself. The Lu brothers' self-imposed exile lasted ten long years, a decade in which they steeped themselves in the Confucian classics, in Taoist and Buddhist wisdom books, and in a thorough and detailed history of literature.

During their exile, Lu Chi wrote a *Dialectic of Destruction* describing the causes of the collapse of the Wu empire, an essay especially notable for its caustic tone and bitter assessment of the general incompetence and self-indulgence of the ruling class. Searching for the causes of calamity within himself, Lu finally must call things by the right name, even when that means placing responsibility with the emperor or with the poet's elders. It was writing that could have gotten him killed.

Finally, the two brothers returned north at the court's direction in 290 as the new court began to decentralize the government. In Lo-yang, Lu Chi was named to office as a literary secretary. But life at court proved to be a constant struggle, as it did to so very many Chinese poets. He referred to the capital as a "foreign country," but managed to persevere until, in 296, he was appointed to head an army detachment to wage war against the barbarians. A deft, inspiring leader, he served well and before long became a personal secretary to the Emperor. But the Fates were not kind: the Emperor lacked both discipline and imagination, and the country was quickly torn apart by the competitive plottings of the eight princes.

In the year 300, the Prince of Chao began a six-year

open war by destroying the entire palace administration. Lu Chi's troops were confronted by an army led by Meng Chao about ten miles from Lo-yang, and in a heated battle, Lu Chi's forces were so severely decimated that it was said corpses dammed the Yangtze River. Lu Chi was charged with treason, given a summary hearing, and executed. As were both of his sons. Lu Chi was forty-two.

He left some 300 poems and essays. Although well-acquainted with the literati of his period, he was, apparently, a decidedly private man who numbered no close friends other than his younger brother, perhaps because of his biting criticism. He said of Tso Ssu for instance, "The old fool's writing a *fu* on each of the three capitals, but when he's done, they'll be good for nothing but wrapping a wine jug in."

Suspicious of fads and literary reputations, he spent a lifetime studying the *Shih Ching* (Classic of Poetry), the *Lun Yu, I Ching*, and the Taoist sages Chuang Tzu and Lao Tzu. Echoes of these classics abound in the *Wen Fu*. He lived in a society in which theology held virtually no sway. Although Buddhism had been imported from India in the first century, the Chinese mind held to practical social matters for the most part, joining aspects of Buddhist wisdom-teaching to practical Confucianism, just as it had made a marriage of Confucianism and Taoism. Only a hundred years later, under the inspired translations of Kumarajiva, would Buddhism — and especially *ch'an* or zen — flower and flourish in China.

"History" as a subject had been born with the

composition of the *Tso Chuan*, a long commentary mixing history and fiction and prophecy, in the fourth century B.C. But Chinese block printing would not be invented until the Sui dynasty, some 300 years after Lu Chi's death. Nor, as noted, was there any *ars poetica* available for Lu Chi to study. Books—in the form of scrolls—were everywhere evident, however, and much in demand. An "educated man" was expected to know the contents of "five cart-loads of books." And because the first emperor of the Ch'in dynasty (200 B.C.) had attempted to purge all books but the *Book of Changes* or *I Ching*, the literate public was constantly protective of its libraries of irreplaceable scrolls.

To this seriousness, Lu adds a *hsin*, "heart/mind," which is unifying. Emotion and reason become one in the fully integrated personality. His culture recognized no distinction between poetry and reason. Nor did the classical Chinese literary mind distinguish between the rational and the irrational. The methodology of Kung was rooted in what we in the West might call the Socratic Tradition. And it is this style of inquiry Lu Chi brings to his rhymed poem on the art and use of letters. His lines are the lines of philosophy and aesthetics, irregular in length and rhythm, and rhymed—and called rhymed-prose or *fu*.

Lu Chi's *fu* is that of the *p'ien wen* or Double Harness style; the poem depends upon a kind of parallelism, often moving two ways simultaneously through the deliberate use of ambiguity: "Things move into shadows and vanish; memory returns in an echo." Lu nonetheless grounds his warnings and urgings in concrete imagery, often drawing on the reader's assumed familiarity with Chinese music and or literary classics.

The word *wen* is among the oldest words in Chinese, going back at least 3,000 years to the time of early shamanism and the oracle bones where it meant, even then, *art*—meaning literary or plastic arts. In its most generic interpretation, *wen* means simply pattern wherein meaning and form become inseparably united, so that they become one, indistinguishable. Furthermore, *wen* means "writing" or "literature" in the context of its being the most natural means of expression of the essential *hsin* (heart/mind) at the core of consciousness. And it was often used to mean "culture" in the broadest sense. Just as Lu's discourse carries certain social connotations and implications, so his choice of the word *wen* carries a plurisignation; he calls forth the term to mean, specifically, literary arts; but literary arts cannot be entirely separated from social responsibilities to, for instance, tell the truth, which in Confucian society means to name things and events properly.

Stephen Owen's elegant study, *Traditional Chinese Poetry and Poetics* (University of Wisconsin, 1985), says this: "In formulation literature is not truly mimetic: rather it is the final stage in a process of manifestation; and the writer, instead of 're-presenting' the outer world, is in fact only the medium for this last phase of the world's coming-to-be." A poet seeks personal *and* social transformation through poetry; the poet's "art" is both a gift *to* the writer and *from* the writer who understands that no great gift can be truly given or received in an emotional or intellectual void. All this is present in Lu Chi's own prose poem on the coming-to-be-ness of a true writer.

By the time of the *Wen Fu*, China had already been two hundred years under the *san chiao* or "Three Doctrines" system. Buddhism, introduced in the first century A.D., was the only true religion of the three, and, during Lu Chi's lifetime, the least influential. Taoism, like Confucianism, was also a philosophy, but loaded with mystical rites and transcendental aspirations. And like Confucianism, it had become corrupted by the creation of vast bureaucracies and social conventions and the rigors and demoralizing struggles of bogus gurus. Taoism also harbored its fortune-tellers and crypto-occultists, witches and daemons.

Lu Chi appears to have concentrated his studies on the virtues of the each of the three, preferring to ignore bureaucratic hierarchies, addressing the Taoist sense of *tzu-chan*, the idea of spontaneous origins as the core inspiration of the process of writing. What we call the Void is only Mind. Daily discipline becomes—in practice—daily life. And yet each day is new. In his insistence upon the right words in the right order, he followed the principles of Master Kung. Spiritually, he reflects a tradition that would evolve into the *ch'an* line of Buddhism. In attitude and in moral turpitude, he drew once again from the strengths of the *san-chiao* system, finding no apparent contradiction between his role as military leader and his inner scholarly and spiritual life.

In the early 1950s, North American readers were

treated to several re-inventions of Lu Chi's famous treatise. E.R. Hughes published a large study which included a translation (Pantheon Books), but unfortunately failed – in the translation at least – to follow much of the advice of its author. Achilles Fang published a translation in the *New Mexico Quarterly* in the fall of 1952, and that same year, Shih-Hsiang Chen published yet another translation in an edition of 400 copies at the Anthoesen Press in Portland, Maine, and reprinted in Cyril Birch's *Anthology of Chinese Literature* (Grove Press, 1965).

These versions, along with Ezra Pound's famous comments on the Preface to the *Wen Fu*, have attracted and inspired many and various poets, including the title poem to Gary Snyder's *Axe Handles*, a poem "correcting" Ezra Pound's translation. But, as Lu Chi himself would be quick to point out, when cutting an axe handle with an axe, the model may indeed be at hand, as he says in the Preface, but the new axe handle, despite being modeled on the old, will be different. Lu Chi directs us to look for the obvious model, knowing that no matter what we do with it, the fruits of our labors will differ from the original. Lu Chi's comments on axe handles come directly from the *Shih Ching, Book I.*

Howard Nemirov's poem, "To Lu Chi," Eleanor Wilner's poem, "Meditation on the Wen Fu," and the title poem of Carolyn Kizer's 1965 collection, *Knock Upon Silence*, all result from readings of those early translations.

In 1987, Jan and Crispin Elsted at the Barbarian Press (Lu Chi would be proud to be published by Barbarians!)

printed a beautiful limited edition of an early version of my translation of the *Wen Fu*, a version that was reprinted in a trade edition that same year by Breitenbush Books. For this (revised, final) edition, I have corrected several errors and misreadings pointed out by friends and scholars, and have, I hope, clarified the text. Among the major revisions, the reader will find a completely revised lineation. This I have done in part out of respect for the Chinese use of the basic couplet form, and in part to achieve a more lyrical structure for the sounding of the text.

Elegant simplicity and common sense, two of the rarest of attributes, distinguish Lu Chi's poem. It was never my intention to offer a strictly literal version of the *Wen Fu* — much of the language of the original is simply mystifying to the average western reader — but to revision the poem in a western lyric mode, to make it as I imagined Lu Chi would if he were Lu Chi in the process of re-inventing himself in another language and culture. This is of course a dangerous mode of procedure, but one followed by poets as early as those of the *Greek Anthology*, Catullus, and indeed Lu Chi himself in his own borrowings and interpretations from the *Shih Ching*, the *Lun Yu*, and dozens of other sources. A few centuries after Lu Chi, the Japanese called this practice *honkadori*, as it came to mean borrowings or deliberate echoes of classical poems. The Chinese no doubt have a similar term.

In practice, I've constructed a lyric paraphrase concentrating on what I perceive to be the primary passages and images. In some places, I've condensed; in

others, it has been necessary to make leaps or to slightly re-
organize. If what I've made is of no *practical* use, I shall
have offered Lu Chi—and myself—no honor. And if these
lines are indeed illuminating to one who struggles over a
word or line, then due credit belongs not only with Lu Chi,
but with his commentators, both Asian and Western, from
whom I've learned.

For additional scholarship, the E.R. Hughes volume
mentioned above is the most substantial scholarly
commentary in English, but loaded with dull language and
academic musing; translations by Shih-Hsiang Chen and
Achilles Fang tend toward the quite literal, and also deeply
reward comparative study.

I am grateful to Emilie Buchwald at Milkweed Editions
for encouraging this revision, and for bringing Lu Chi back
into the English-speaking world. Special thanks are also due
to Tree Swenson, my partner and publisher at Copper
Canyon Press, for her unfailing efforts to afford an obscure
poet time to write and translate and for her unflagging
moral support; and to William O'Daly, sometime editor and
full-time confidant.

A hundred years after Lu Chi composed his *Wen Fu*, the
reclusive poet T'ao Ch'ien (also called T'ao Yuan-ming)
wrote a poem to his cousin, saying:

> Reading the classics again,
> sometimes I still find heroes,

old sages I dare not emulate,
but who stood strong in adversity.

I too will not choose the easy way.

His poem echoes the advice of Lu Chi. He finds heroes he
"dares not emulate" but who nonetheless set models and
standards, both literary and ethical. Studying the "working
of the minds" of these heroes, he clarifies his own thinking
and thereby underscores his determination to follow within
a defined tradition. In the preface to his poem, "The
Return," he says, "Whenever I have been involved in official
life I was mortgaging myself to my mouth and belly, and
the realization of this greatly upset me. I was deeply
ashamed that I had so compromised my principles."
(Translated by James Robert Hightower, *The Poetry of T'ao
Ch'ien*, Oxford University Press, 1970.) Just as Lu Chi chose
to "bar the door" for a ten-year period of intense study,
T'ao Ch'ien left "official life" to return to his poor farm, his
wife and children often facing hunger, poverty, and political
tribulations, but his principles intact.

Both T'ao Ch'ien's bravery and his profound ethical
accountability follow in the Confucian/Taoist tradition Lu
Chi so luminously espoused. Lu Chi and T'ao Ch'ien set
standards that would be followed by Tu Fu and other major
Chinese poets, and the *Wen Fu* remains as fresh, and as
demanding, for us some seventeen centuries later as it was
for the great T'ao Ch'ien.

Lu Chi was not interested in fostering a "writing school"

or in establishing himself as the leader of any particular literary movement. His aim was to articulate the ethical and spiritual lineage of great writers, to connect himself with predecessors for whom the art of writing was neither easy nor self-serving, to articulate the whole inner life of the writer and the tradition.

–Sam Hamill
Port Townsend, 1990

Wen Fu

The Art of Writing

When studying the work of the Masters,
    I watch the working of their minds.

Surely, facility with language
    and the charging of the word with energy

are effects which can be achieved
    by various means.

Still, the beautiful can be distinguished
    from the common,
    the good from the mediocre.

Only through writing and then revising
    and revising
    may one gain the necessary insight.

We worry whether our ideas
    may fall short of their subjects,
    whether form and content rhyme.

This may be easy to know,
    but it is difficult to put into practice.

I have composed this rhymed prose
    on the *Ars Poetica* to introduce

27

past masterpieces as models
    for an examination
    of the good and the bad in writing.

Perhaps it will one day be said
    that I have written something of substance,

something useful,
    that I have entered the Mystery.

When cutting an axe handle with an axe,
    surely the model is at hand.

Each writer finds a new entrance into the Mystery,
    and it is difficult to explain.

Nonetheless, I have set down my thinking
    as clearly as I am able.

I. The Early Motion

The poet stands at the center of the universe,
    contemplating the enigma,

drawing sustenance
    from masterpieces of the past.

Studying the four seasons as they pass,
    we sigh;

seeing the inner-connectedness of things,
    we learn the innumerable ways of the world.

We mourn leaves torn away
    by the cruel hands of autumn;

we honor every tender bud of spring.

Autumn frost sends a shudder through the heart;
    summer clouds can make the spirit soar.

Learn to recite the classics;
    sing in the clear virtue of ancient masters;

explore the treasures of the classics
where form and content are born.

Thus moved, I lay aside my books
and take writing brush in hand
to make this composition.

II. Beginning

Eyes closed, we listen
    to inner music,
    lost in thought and question:

our spirits ride
    to the eight corners of the universe,
    mind soaring a thousand miles away;

only then may the inner voice
    grow clear
    as objects become numinous.

We pour forth the essence of words,
    savoring their sweetness.

It is like being adrift
    in a heavenly lake
    or diving to the depths of seas.

We bring up living words
    like fishes
    hooked in their gills, leaping from the deep.

Luminous words are brought down
    like a bird on an arrowstring
    shot from passing clouds.

We gather words and images
    from those unused by previous generations.

Our melodies have been unplayed
    for a thousand years or more.

The morning blossoms bloom;
    soon, the night buds will unfold.

Past and present commingle:
Eternity in the single blink of an eye!

III. Choosing Words

Ordering thoughts and ideas,
    we begin to choose our words.

Each choice is made with care,
    fit with a sense of proportion.

Shadowy thoughts are brought into the light of reason;
    echoes are traced to their sources.

It is like following a branch to find the trembling leaf,
    like following a stream to find the spring.

The poet brings light into great darkness, even if that means
    the simple become difficult or the difficult easy.

Hence, the tiger may silence others beasts,
    the dragon frighten away birds in terrifying waves.

Writing, the traveling is sometimes level and easy,
    sometime rocky and steep.

Calm the heart's dark waters;
    collect from deep thoughts the proper names for things.

Heaven and earth are trapped in visible form:
    all things emerge from the writing brush.

At first, the brush parches our lips,
    but soon it grows moist from dipping.

Truth is the tree-trunk;
    style makes beautiful foliage.

Emotion and reason are not two things:
    every shift in feeling must be read.

Finding true joy, find laughter;
    in sorrow, identify each sigh.

Sometimes the words come freely;
    sometimes we sit in silence, gnawing on a brush.

IV. The Satisfaction

The pleasure a writer knows
    is the pleasure of Sages.

Out of non-being, being is born;
    out of silence, a writer produces a song.

In a single yard of silk, there is infinite space;
    language is a deluge from one small corner of the heart.

The net of images is cast wider and wider;
    thought searches more and more deeply.

The writer offers the fragrance of fresh flowers,
    an abundance of sprouting buds.

Bright winds lift each metaphor;
clouds lift from a forest of writing brushes.

V. Catalogue of Genres

A body of writing may take any of a thousand forms,
    and there is no one right way to measure.

Changing, changing at the flick of a hand,
    its various forms are almost impossible to capture.

Words and phrases may compete with one another,
    but the mind is master.

Caught between the unborn and the living,
    a writer struggles to maintain both depth and surface.

One may depart from the square or overstep the circle
    searching for the one true form of a particular reality.

A writer fills a reader's eyes with splendor
    and clarifies values.

One whose language remains muddled cannot do it;
    only when held in a clear mind can the language
    become noble.

The lyric [shih] articulates speechless emotion, creating a
    fabric.
Rhymed prose [fu] presents its objects clearly.
Inscriptions [pei] must be simply written.

Elegies [lei] contain tangled webs of grief and should be
    kept mournful.
Mnemonic poems [ming] must be simple, but must also be
    pregnant with meaning.
Admonitions [chen] cut against the grain and should
    therefore be written directly.
Eulogies [sung] are praises, but must demonstrate balance.
The treatise [lun] should be subtle, smooth, and polished.
Memorials [tsou] are simple and quiet, but carry a highly
    polished elegance.
The discourse [shuo] should be both radiant and cunning.

Although each form is different, each opposes evil:
    and none grants a writer license.

Language must speak from its essence to articulate reason:
verbosity indicates lack of virtue.

VI. On Harmony

Each new composition assumes a special air,
    but only through trying many shapes and changes,
    learning the art of the subtle.

Ideas seek harmonious existence, one among others,
    through language that is both beautiful and true.

Sounds interlock and intermingle
    like the five colors of embroidery,
    each enhancing the others.

While it is true emotions are often capricious,
    indulgence is self-destructive.

Recognizing order
    is like opening a dam in a river.

Not-knowing is like grabbing the tail
    to direct the head of the dragon.

When dark and light are poorly mixed,
the only result is muddy.

VII. On Revision

Looking back, search for the disharmonious image;
    anticipating what may come,
    prepare for a smooth transition.

Even with right reason, the words
    will sometimes clang; sometimes language flows,
    though the ideas themselves remain trivial.

Know one from the other
    and the writing will be clearer;
    confuse the two, and everything will suffer.

Art and virtue are measured in tiny grains.

The general inspects his men
    for every minutest detail,
    down to a single hair.

Only when revisions are precise
may the building stand square and plumb.

VII. The Key

While the language may be lovely
    and the reasoning just,

the ideas themselves
    may prove trivial.

What wants to continue must not end;
    what has been fully stated is itself a conclusion.

However each sentence branches and spreads,
    it grows from a well-placed phrase.

Restrain verbosity, establish order;
otherwise, further and further revision.

IX. On Originality

The mind weaves elaborate tapestries
    with elegant, multi-colored foliage.

The composition must move the heart
    like music from an instrument with many strings.

There are no new ideas,
    only those which rhyme with certain classics.

The shuttle has worked in my heart
    as it worked the hearts of those who came before me;

continuing the same warp and woof,
    I must make my fabric new.

Where truth and virtue are threatened,
I must surrender even my favorite jewels.

X. Shadow and Echo and Jade

Perhaps only a single blossom
    from the whole bouquet will bloom.

Perhaps only a single, lonely cornstalk
    rises in the field.

Shadows cannot be held;
    echoes cannot be harnessed.

Poor work is an eyesore and obvious:
    it cannot be woven into music.

When the mind is caged and separate,
    the spirit wanders
    and nothing is controlled.

When the vein of jade is revealed in the rock,
    the whole mountain glistens.

Images must shine
    like pearls in water;

the thorn-bush, left unpruned,
    spreads in glorious disarray.

A common song sung to a great melody
is another way to find beauty.

XI. Five Criteria

1. *Music*

When the rhythm is slack and has no tradition,
the poem falters.

The poet searches in the silence for a friend,
but finds none.

The poet calls and calls into the Void,
but nothing answers.

Heaven is out of reach—
vast and empty.

A single weak note plucked on a lute
cannot make beautiful music.

2. *Harmony*

When the phrasing is lazy or self-indulgent,
    the music is gaudy,
    and no one will find beauty.

Where the beautiful mingles with the common,
    it is the beautiful that suffers.

One small blemish
    mars the whole beautiful face.

It is like hearing a harsh note
    from a flute from the courtyard below:
    it resonates out of tune.

One can make music
and still lack all harmony.

3. *True Emotion*

Searching for a subject, a poet may indulge
    in the needlessly obscure or in the trivial,
    forsaking common sense.

Then *all* words will lack grace,
    they will ramble,
    and love will be betrayed.

As with the thinnest chords of the lute,
    one detects music and harmony
    that is present, yet resists definition.

Even though in tune,
the music may fail in its mission.

4. *Restraint*

Sometimes rhythms and harmonies dominate
    and the poet finds them seductive.

Or, enchanted by the poet's voice,
    the crowd may shout hosannahs.

Then vanity floods the eyes with the vulgar–
    a pretentious tune
    is unsuited to disciplined emotion.

It is like a bad musician who,
    to drown out imperfections,
    plays too loudly.

False feelings are a slap
    in the face of grace.

Even disciplined feeling leads nowhere
unless there is also refinement.

5. *Refinement*

Only when the poem is free of false emotion and confusion
   will the passions come into perspective.

Even then, the poem may be blander than sacrificial broth;
   it may be a blurred note from a broken string.

Hyper-aware of technique, the poem may be stripped
   of its seasoning like a feast without gravy.

Or it may be good enough for "one to sing, three to praise"
and still lack grace.

XII. Finding Form

Know when the work
    should be full,

and when it should be
    compacted.

Know when to lift your eyes
    and when to scrutinize.

Adapt to occasions as they arise;
    permit emotions to be subtle.

Even when the language is common,
    the images must be telling.

When the thinking is clumsy,
    the language must move very smoothly.

Old clothes
    can be refurbished;

the stream we muddy
    soon runs itself clean again.

Only after looking and listening
    closely

can one make these various subtleties
     work magic.

The sleeves of the dancers
     move with the melodies;

the singers' voices rise
     and fall with the music.

P'ien the Wheelwright
     tried to explain it,
     but he couldn't.

Nor can the artificial flowers of the critics explain it.

XIII. The Masterpiece

I take the rules of grammar and guides to good language
  and clutch them to my heart and mind.

Know what is and what is not
  merely fashion;

learn what old masters praised highly,

although the wisdom of a subtle mind
  may be scoffed at by the public.

The brilliant semi-precious stones of popular fashion
  are as common as beans in the field.

Though the writers of my generation
  produce in profusion,

all their real jewels cannot
  fill the cup I make of my fingers.

As infinite as space, good work
  joins earth to heaven;

it comes from nothing,
  like air through a bellows.

We carry the bucket from the well,
    but the bucket soon is empty.

Wanting every word to sing,
    every writer worries:

nothing is ever perfect;
    no poet can afford to become complacent.

We hear a jade bell's laughter
    and think it laughs at us.

For a poet, there is terror in the dust.

XIV. The Terror

I worry that my ink well
    may run dry,

that right words
    cannot be found.

I want to respond to each
    moment's inspiration.

Work with what is given;
    that which passes cannot be detained.

Things move into shadows and vanish;
    memory returns in an echo.

When Spring arrives,
    we understand why Nature has reasons.

Thoughts rise from the heart on breezes
    and language finds its speaker.

Yesterday's buds are this morning's blossoms
    we draw with a brush on silk.

Every eye knows a pattern;
every ear hears distant music.

XV. The Inspiration

The time comes when emotions strangle,
    though every stimulus wants response;

there are times
    when the spirit freezes.

The writer feels dead as bleached wood,
    dry as a riverbed in drought.

For a way out, search the depths of the soul
    for a spirit;

beg, if need be,
    for a sign of life.

The dark inside of the mind
    lies hidden;

thoughts must be brought like a child
    from the womb,
        terrified and screaming.

Forcing emotions brings error
    and error again;

letting them come naturally
means letting them come clear.

The truth of the thing lies inside us,
but no power on earth can force it.

Time after time,
I search my heart in this struggle.

Sometimes a door slowly opens;
sometimes the door remains bolted.

XVI. Conclusion

Consider the use of letters.
All principles demand them.

Though they travel a thousand miles or more,
nothing in this world can stop them.

They traverse
the thousands of years.

Look at them one way,
and they clarify laws for the future.

Look at them another,
and they provide models from old masters.

The art of letters has saved governments from ruin
and propagates morals.

Through letters, there is no road
too difficult to travel,

no idea too confusing
to be ordered.

It comes like rain from clouds;
it renews the vital spirit.

Inscribed on bronze and marble,
it honors every virtue.

It sings in flute and strings
and every day is made newer.

Cover Image:

The ancient Chinese "patron saint" of letters, Kuei Hsing was renowned for great writing but cursed with a repugnant countenance. When it came time for the Emperor to hand out literary certification at the capital, he found Kuei Hsing unbearable to look at. The poet was so humiliated that he threw himself into the river to drown. But he was carried into the heavens by a magical fish to live in a palace in the Big Dipper where he became the arbiter of literature and calligraphy.

Wen Fu was designed by R.W. Scholes and typeset in 13 point Perpetua at Stanton Publication Services.